HEINEMANN

SECONDARY

HISTORY

PROJECT

THE USA

1919–1941

FOUNDATION EDITION

Jane Shuter

Heinemann

Heinemann Educational Publishers
Halley Court, Jordan Hill, Oxford OX2 8EJ
a division of Reed Educational and Professional
Publishing Ltd

OXFORD MADRID ATHENS FLORENCE PRAGUE
CHICAGO PORTSMOUTH NH (USA) MEXICO CITY
SAO PAULO SINGAPORE KUALA LUMPUR TOKYO
MELBOURNE AUCKLAND IBADAN NAIROBI
KAMPALA GABORONE JOHANNESBURG

First published 1997

00 99 98 97
10 9 8 7 6 5 4 3 2 1

British Library Cataloguing in Publication data is available
from the British Library on request.

ISBN: 0 435 30901 3

Designed, produced and illustrated by Visual Image
Printed by Mateu Cromo in Spain
Cover Design by The Wooden Ark Studio

Acknowledgements

The publishers would like to thank the following for
permission to reproduce photographs:

William Benton Museum of Art, University of Connecticut
45 below
Corbis UK Ltd   7, 24, 25, 28 top, 31, 35, 40, 43, 45 top, 46, 50,
52, 53, 60
Corbis UK Ltd, Library of Congress   4, 20 left
Corbis UK Ltd, Hulton Deutsch 16
Corbis-Bettmann   6, 37, 42, 63
Corbis-Bettmann/UPI 34
Mary Evans Picture Library   10, 18 above, 22
The Kobal collection   19
Herbert Hoover Presidential Library/Corbis 49
Peter Newark's Western Americana   11, 12, 26, 32, 33, 41, 51
Ohio Historical Society   30
Popperfoto   18 below, 28
Punch Library 58
Topham Picturepoint   20 right, 21

The publishers have made every effort to trace copyright
holders of material in this book. Any omissions will be
rectified in subsequent printings if notice is given to the
publisher.

Details of written sources

In some sources the wording or sentence structure has been
simplified to ensure that the source is accessible.

American Women's Association, *Women Workers through the
Depression*, Norwood Press, 1934: 5.7-5
Paul Avrich, *Sasco and Vanzetti*, Princetown
University Press, 1991: 3.4K
Alben W.Barkley *That Reminds Me*, Garden City
Press, New York, 1954: 5.6C
Alexander Baron, *A Reminiscent History of Prohibition*, 1995:
3.6C
Irving Bernstein, *The New Deal, The worker and the Great
Depression*, Houghton Mifflin, Boston1985: 5.7-2, 4
John F. Bowman, Thomas H. Goode, *In the Eye of the
Depression*, Northern Illinois University Press, 1988: 5.4I
P. Davies and B. Moore (eds), *Cinema, Politics and Society in
America*, Manchester University Press, 1985: 2.3G
Frank Freidel, *America in the Twentieth Century*
Alfred A. Knopf, 1970: 2.2D, 3.7-3, 4.1B, C, 4.4L, 5.1D
William Ivy Hair, *The Kingfish and his Realm*, Louisiana State
University, 1991: 5.6B
Alden P. Hatch, *Franklin D. Roosevelt*, Henry Holt and Co.,
1947: 5.6E
S.M. Harrison, *World Conflict in the Twentieth Century*,
Macmillan, 1987: 4.6-2
C.P. Hill, *Franklin D. Roosevelt and the New Deal*, George
Arnold, 1975: 5.5P
House of Representatives 72nd Congress, *Unemployment in the
US*, Hearings before a sub-committee on labor, 1932: 5.7-3
A. Howarth, *Twentieth Century History*, Longman 1979: 5.1B,
5.5O
Will Irwin, *Herbert Hoover, a Reminiscent Biography*, Century,
1928: 4.6-3
William Leuchtenburg, *Franklin D. Roosevelt and The New Deal*,
Harper and Row, 1963: 5.4K
R. Muller-Freinfels in *America in Perspective*, ed.
Daniel Heath *et.al.*, Houghton Mifflin, 1986: 1.1A
Michael Parrish, *Anxious Decades: America in Prosperity and
Decline 1920-41*, W.W. Norton and Co., 1992: 3.3F, 3.3I, 3.4L,
3.5M, 3.6A, 3.7-2, 4.2E
Albert V. Romasco, *The Poverty of Abundance*, OUP 1965: 4.6-1
Arthur Schlesinger, *The Age of Roosevelt, The Coming of the New
Deal*, William Heinemann, 1960: 5.4J
D. Snowman, *America since 1920, the Effects of the Depression*,
Heinemann, 1968: 2.3H, 4.4N
Harriet Ward, *World Powers in the Twentieth Century*,
Heinemann, 1978: 2.5-7

CONTENTS

CHAPTER 1   THIS IS THE UNITED STATES

1.1	The United States as a major power	5
1.2	The people of the United States of America	6
1.3	The Government of the United States	8

CHAPTER 2   THE USA IN THE 1920S – THE GOOD TIMES

2.1	The economic boom	10
2.2	Investing in the stock market	13
2.3	Changing life styles	14
2.4	Case Study - the Hollywood greats?	18
2.5	Exercise: Boom time in the United States	20

CHAPTER 3   THE USA IN THE 1920S – THE BAD TIMES

3.1	Isolationism	22
3.2	The economic failures	24
3.3	Racism and Black rights	26
3.4	Red scares and Religious Fundamentalism	29
3.5	Prohibition	30
3.6	Case Study ~ Alphonse Capone, 'Gangster Number 1'	32
3.7	Exercise: The enforcement of prohibition	34

CHAPTER 4   THE USA AND THE STOCK MARKET CRASH

4.1	What was the Wall Street Crash?	36
4.2	Why did the Wall Street Crash happen?	38
4.3	What were the effects of the Wall Street Crash?	40
4.4	The Great Depression in the United States	42
4.5	Case Study: President Hoover and the Depression	46
4.6	Exercise: Herbert Hoover – does he deserve the criticism he has attracted?	48

CHAPTER 5   ROOSEVELT AND THE NEW DEAL

5.1	Why did Roosevelt win the 1932 election?	50
5.2	The New Deal in action	52
5.3	The main Alphabet Agencies	55
5.4	How successful was the New Deal?	56
5.5	Opposition to the New Deal	58
5.6	Case Study – Huey Long, Governor of Louisiana	60
5.7	Exercise: Unemployment in the 1930s – snapshots of despair	62

	INDEX	64

CHAPTER 1

THIS IS THE UNITED STATES

▲ In 1919 the United States had 48 states. In 1959 Alaska and Hawaii joined, making 50 states altogether.

A huge country

The United States of America (USA) is huge, over 30 times the size of Great Britain. In 1919 it had three cities (New York, Philadelphia and Chicago) with a population of over one million. Great Britain had only one – London.

Natural resources

By 1920 America was the largest industrial country in the world. Almost 40% of the world's **manufactured** goods (goods made in factories) came from America. Lots of natural resources (like oil, coal and food) helped America's industries to grow.

▲ The 'Stars and Stripes'. Each star stands for a state. The stripes stand for the first 13 colonies.

A world power?

America had also begun to take over other countries. It controlled islands in the Pacific Ocean. It also controlled the Panama Canal, which links the Atlantic and Pacific Oceans.

Benefiting from the First World War

America did not enter the First World War until 1917, three years after it started. But, once in, America's huge resources tipped the balance in favour of the Allies (Britain, France and Russia) and helped bring about Germany's defeat.

The war gave a big boost to the American economy. American banks lent the Allies huge sums of money. They used a lot of this money to buy American-made equipment for their troops. The war disrupted trade and food production in Europe. American farmers sold food to Europe. They used the money they made from this to expand their farms. American companies took over Europe's world trade.

Source A

America is not a country like Germany – it is a continent. When you travel across the country, you have to keep setting your watch back. When it is 12pm in New York, it is 11am in Chicago, 10am in Denver and 9am in Los Angeles.

Asking if you should visit Yellowstone Park and California is like asking a man travelling in Europe if he will also visit Leningrad and Egypt.

▲ Said by a German visiting America in 1927.

A mixture of people

The first people in the USA were Native American Indians. From the 1500s, a stream of people left Europe to live in the USA. Leaving one country to live in another is called **emigration**. When people move to a new country they are called **immigrants** to that country.

The Native American Indians were moved off their lands to make room for the new immigrants. They did not want to go. Many of them were killed in wars against the immigrants. As more and more people came to the USA, the Native American Indians were pushed off more and more land. Most of them still live in special areas, called 'reservations', set up for them by the government.

The 'Open Door'

At first, the American government made it easy for people to enter the country. Until 1915, all that you had to do to live in America was to find a way of getting there. America's door was open to all.

The American Dream

The people who emigrated to the USA in the early 1900s did so for many reasons. Russian Jews went to get away from persecution over their religion. Other people were escaping from poverty. They all saw America as the land of opportunity. They believed that hard-working people would succeed there, no matter where they came from. This was called the 'American Dream'.

▼ A cartoon from 1891. Uncle Sam (a symbol of the USA) looking at new immigrants.

Source B

Who made it?

Immigrants such as Andrew Carnegie (see Source C) showed the American Dream could come true. Carnegie's family emigrated to the USA from Scotland in 1847. Andrew worked and saved and eventually built up a steel company worth over $250,000,000.

For most immigrants, the American Dream never came true. Most of them ended up living in slums. The only work they could find was in 'sweatshop' industries – where they worked long hours for low pay. America was getting richer, but many Americans were struggling to make a living. In 1919, 1% of Americans had half the country's money. Many others were very poor.

Shutting the door?

By 1914 Americans were a wide variety of races, colours, religions and cultures. Some people began to resent the **Open Door policy**. They saw new immigrants as a threat. In 1917 Congress passed an Act saying that all immigrants had to pass a test to see if they could read and write before they could come to live in America.

The quota system

In 1921 an Immigration Act was passed introducing the **quota system**. This said that only 357,000 immigrants would be allowed to enter America each year (compared with a rate of over a million a year at the time).

In 1924 another Immigration Act limited new immigrants to 164,000 each year. The Open Door into the United States had been firmly closed.

Source C

▲ Andrew Carnegie (1835-1919). By 1900 his steel business was making a quarter of all American steel.

Source D

The immigrants already here regulate immigration. When there are lots of jobs, they send for their relatives. When jobs are scarce, they hold back.

There is no 'immigrant problem'. We have problems of child labour, unemployment, accidents at work. They will not be solved by restricting or prohibiting immigration.

▲ A US immigrant commenting in 1912 on the idea that immigration should be limited.

How is America run?
The American system of government was set up in 1787. In that year, thirteen British colonies broke free from British rule to form the United States. They wrote a **constitution** – a set of rules for running the country. That constitution still forms the basis of the way that modern America is governed, although there have been 26 changes or additions to it.

Federal Government
The federal government in Washington, led by the President, makes important decisions about relations with other countries, defence and the economy. federal laws apply all over America. A special court, the Supreme Court, makes sure Federal laws do not break the constitution.

State Government
Each state has its own government, led by the State Governor. State governments make laws about education, local taxes and law and order. This is why the death penalty only exists in some states.

Who gets elected?
The United States is a democracy. The people **elect** (vote to choose) the people who run the country. In most states they also elect people like the town mayor, local judges and the police chief.

The House of Representatives
Each state elects congressmen to represent them in the **House of Representatives**. Different states elect different numbers of congressmen. The more people there are in a state, the more congressmen they can elect. In 1988, California had 45 congressmen, New York had 34 and Alaska had one.

The Senate and Congress
Every state elects two senators to represent them in the **Senate**. The Senate and the House of Representatives meet in **Congress**, to make federal laws.

The President
Each political party chooses people to run as President and Vice-President. Americans elect one of these pairs every four years.

QUESTIONS

Use the text and sources on pages 4–8 to answer the following questions.

1 How did the First World War affect America's economy?

2 List some reasons why people emigrated to the United States in the early twentieth century?

3 'Source B on page 6 shows that Americans have always disliked immigrants'. Do you agree? Explain your answer.

4 Think about how the USA began. How might this explain why America has federal and state laws and governments?

THE PRESIDENT

The President is elected for 4 years and is head of the Federal Government.
He may veto (refuse to accept) any law passed by Congress,
unless it has a 2/3 majority.

CONSTITUTION

The laws drawn up in 1787 for running
the USA. Each change to the
constitution is called an amendment.

THE SUPREME COURT

Nine Judges who are the highest court
in the US, and also have the power to
declare any State or Federal laws as
unconstitutional – against the American
constitution.

CONGRESS

Congress is the law-making
body in the U.S. It is divided
into the Senate and the
House of Representatives.

HOUSE OF REPRESENTATIVES

Each state elects a
number of congressmen
(depending on the
population of the state)
for 2 years.

SENATE

Each state elects two
Senators to serve for
either 2 or 6 years.

STATE GOVERNMENT

Each state elects a Governor, usually from
one of the two major political parties.
Other officials are also elected.

POLITIAL PARTIES

The President, congressmen and senators are
usually elected from one of the two major parties:
The Democrats and the Republicans.

▲ The Government of the United States.

CHAPTER 2

THE USA IN THE 1920s – THE GOOD TIMES

The 'Roaring Twenties'

After the First World War, controlling world trade made America a rich country. The economy was booming. American industry made huge profits. Many people could afford to buy cars, radios and other 'luxury' goods for the first time. The 1920s were exciting times.

People had money to spare and more free time. They went to sporting events. They went to movies – a new entertainment which sparked off a whole new industry. Women had worked and had more freedom during the First World War. Many did not want to give this up.

2.1 The economic boom

An **economic boom** is when industry does well. Factories make and sell a lot of goods. This makes money, which is put back into the factories, to make more goods, to sell more, to make even more money.

Source A

◄ An assembly line making cars in 1929.

During the 1920s America's industries expanded rapidly. There were many reasons for this:

- **Mass production:** More and more factories used **assembly lines** to produce goods faster and in huge quantities. So, in a car assembly line, each worker did a number of small jobs as the car moved along the line. This was quick and efficient. Making all cars the same also helped cut costs. Henry Ford said about the cars from his factory: 'You can have any colour you like, so long as its black'.

  By 1930, the big car firms (Chrysler, Ford and General Motors) had made 23 million cars using mass production. That was almost one for each American family.

- **Money to lend** During the 1920s the money the USA had lent to the Allies during the First World War was paid back with **interest** (a charge for borrowing the money). So, banks had plenty of money to lend to people who wanted to build new factories.

- **Advertising** Advertisers tried hard to talk Americans into buying consumer goods. They used radio, newspapers, magazines and billboards to push people to buy more goods.

- **Hire-purchase** How could people pay for all these goods? The 1920s was when hire-purchase began. Goods were paid for in **instalments** – a bit at a time. If you did not have to pay all at once, you could buy more. About half of the consumer goods sold in the 1920s were paid for by hire-purchase.

THE IMPORTANCE OF THE MOTOR CAR TO AMERICAN INDUSTRY IN THE 1920s

- Between 1920 and 1929, 15 million cars were made.
- In the 1920s almost 400,000 km of surfaced roads were built and road builders were America's biggest employers.
- By 1929 three-quarters of America's production of plate glass, leather and rubber was used in the car industry.
- By 1929 the jobs of over four million workers depended on the car industry.

▼ A poster advertising the Sears, Roebuck mail order catalogue of 1927.

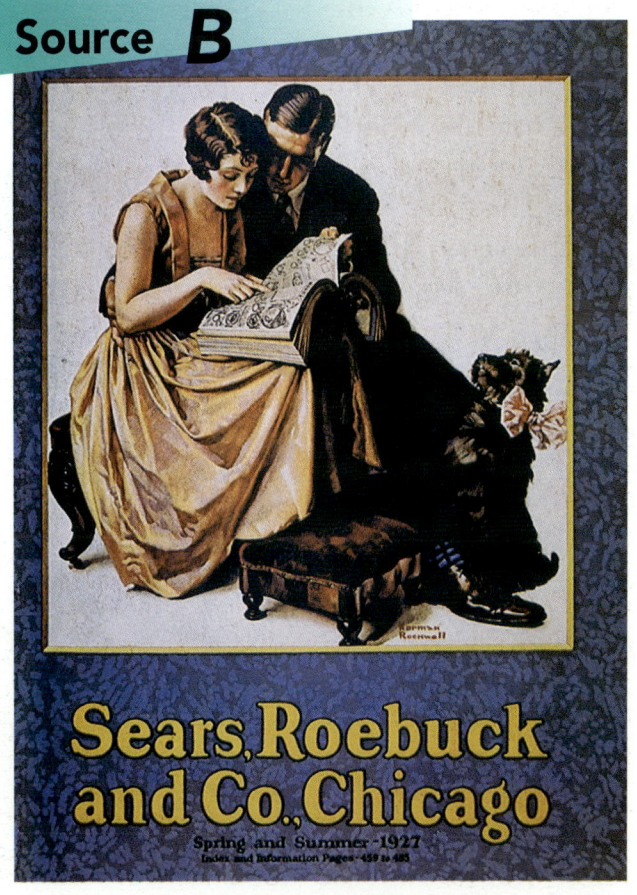

Source B

Sears, Roebuck and Co., Chicago

Spring and Summer 1927
Index and Information Pages 459 to 485

- **Low taxation** The government kept taxes low. So businesses kept more of the profit they made. They used this to build new, efficient factories which made cheaper goods. During the 1920s business profits rose by 80%. Some people became millionaires. Many workers' wages went up too.

- **Tariffs** In 1922 the government put high **tariffs** (special charges) on foreign goods brought into the USA. Foreign companies had to raise the price of their goods to pay the tariffs. So American goods became cheaper than foreign goods. So more Americans bought goods made in American factories.

Source C

▼ A Model T Ford in 1923.

- **Confidence** A big reason for the success of industry in the USA was the confidence of the American people. Business people had the confidence to invest in new factories, sure they would make money. Consumers had the confidence to buy goods on hire-purchase. So factories **did** make money.

QUESTIONS

1 Make a list of the reasons why an economic boom happened in America in the 1920s.

2 How did mass production help the American economy in the 1920s?

3 What did the government do to help the economic boom of the 1920s?

SUMMARY

Factors in the economic boom in the United States

▶ Mass production

▶ Plentiful finance

▶ Advertising

▶ Hire-purchase

▶ Low taxation

▶ Tariffs on foreign goods

▶ Consumer confidence

When a company is set up it raises money by selling **shares** in itself. **Shareholders**, the people who buy shares in the company, make money in two ways. Firstly, they get a share of the profits the company makes each year. This is called a **dividend**. Secondly, they can sell the shares. If a company is successful, the price of its shares go up.

Shareholders could sell shares for more than they paid for them. In the 1920s, more and more Americans bought shares. Some people borrowed money from banks to buy shares. They sold the shares at a profit, paid the bank and had money left. This was called 'buying on the margin'.

▼ Buying shares 'On the margin'

Getting rich quick?

There was a problem with buying on the margin. It seemed like a way of getting rich quick, but it could be dangerous. What if the prices of shares stopped going up? What if they went down? People who had borrowed money from banks would not be able to pay off the money they had borrowed to buy shares. People were too confident about the American economy to think this might happen. Even the financial experts seemed to think the boom would go on forever.

2.3 Changing lifestyles

Source E

More time for fun

Labour-saving devices for the home, like washing machines, gave people more free time. Mass production meant people worked less. Americans began to look for ways of filling their spare time.

One very popular way was listening to the radio. Radios were being mass produced cheaply. Many people could afford them. Radio stations sprang up all over the country.

Over 50 million people listened to the radio, which brought them more than just entertainment. Americans who could not read could catch up on the news on radio.

◀ The front cover of *Life* Magazine in 1926. It shows a young girl teaching an old man one of the new fashionable dances.

THE POWER OF RADIO – THE MARTIAN INVASION

On the evening of 30 October 1938, CBS Radio broadcast a play called 'The War of the Worlds'. It was about aliens invading America. It was advertised as a play, but it was very realistic. It used imaginary news broadcasts and interviews with government officials.

Welles, pretending to be a news-reader, said that ten Martian spaceships had landed in New Jersey. He said a reporter had been killed by one of the Martians, armed with a ray gun. He was so convincing that millions believed him!

All across the United States people began to panic. There were so many telephone calls to CBS asking for advice that their phone lines were jammed. Some people had heart attacks. Others had to be treated for shock. No one at CBS had thought that this would happen!

CBS apologised the next day. Orson Welles had to keep out of the way until the fuss died down. He later said, 'I don't think we will try anything like this again!'

Music and dance

The radio brought people news and drama. It also brought them music. The 1920s are sometimes called the 'Jazz Age' because jazz music became popular then. Older people hated jazz, but young Americans loved to listen and dance to it.

Getting around

As more families owned cars, they became much more mobile. Better-off Americans went on weekend trips all over the country. Cars and buses meant that many more people could go to dances, concerts and sporting events. Huge crowds went to baseball, American football and boxing matches in the 1920s.

The movies

The most popular entertainment in the 1920s was the cinema. A visit to the cinema became part of American life. By 1926 there were over 17,000 movie houses, many in small villages.

Until 1927 there were no soundtracks on films. They were 'silent'. A pianist played tunes while the film ran, fast music for chase scenes, romantic music for love scenes, and so on. Film stars, like Charlie Chaplin and Greta Garbo, became famous. In 1926 Greta Garbo earned $5,000 a week – enough to buy ninety Model T Ford cars a year!

In 1927 the first 'talkie' was made. Films had soundtracks for the first time. They became even more popular. The movie industry, based in Hollywood, grew even faster than any other American industry.

By 1930 over 100 million cinema tickets were sold every week. Movie-makers found that sex sold tickets. Newspapers wrote about the lurid love-lives of film stars. Although the 'sexy' movies would seem tame today, many people began to disapprove of all this sex – on and off the screen.

The Hays Code

The Hollywood film studios decided to tighten up. They set up the Hays Office, run by an ex-congressman, Will Hays. He wrote the Hays Code, a set of rules for film-making (see the box on the left). Some actors were sacked for 'improper behaviour'. But, in the long run, the Hays Code made little difference to the cinema.

Source F

▶ A 'flapper' dancing on the table. This is a scene from a film made in the 1920s.

Source G

All the adventure, all the romance, all the excitement you lack in your daily life is in the Pictures. They take you completely out of yourself into a wonderful new world.

Out of the cage of everyday existence: if only for an afternoon or an evening – escape!'

◀ Part of an advertisement for the cinema. It was printed in a made up issue of the *Saturday Evening Post*, used in the film 'Middletown' in 1929.

Women before the First World War

Before the First World War 'respectable' women dressed sensibly. They were polite and were never alone with a man. Everyone expected them to become wives and mothers. Very few women had careers. In most states women did not have the vote.

The First World War and after

During the First World War, women were needed to work in factories making war goods. They showed that women could work as hard and as well as men. The government was grateful. In 1920, women were given the vote in all states. Some of them began to challenge the idea that they had to become the 'little lady at home'. In the cities younger women began to wear shorter skirts and more make-up. Some women, called 'flappers', were famous for partying and wearing outrageous clothes.

Changes for everyone?

Not all women had more freedom. More women had jobs, mainly because women's wages were lower. Not all women wanted to work, or be flappers. And not everyone wanted them to. In many places those who broke away from the old ways were looked down on.

Source H

The flapper had bobbed hair and a pudding basin hat. She wore rouge and lipstick.

She flattened her breasts. She wore waistless, short skirts and flesh coloured stockings.

She was the symbol of the age.

 From *America Since 1920*, D. Snowman, 1968.

SUMMARY

The 1920s – The good times

► Economic boom means people are better off

► Radio and cinema tell people more about the world

► Cars increase mobility

► People have more spare time

► Dancing, music and movies become very popular

► Attitudes to women begin to change

QUESTIONS

1 Read pages 13–14.
   a What was 'buying on the margin'?
   b Why was it risky?
   c Why, then, did so many people do it?

2 What does Source D (page 14) tell us about American attitudes to buying shares in 1929?

3 a List the rules from the Hays Code.
   b Choose one rule. Explain what effect you think it was supposed to have.

RUDOLPH VALENTINO

Rudolph Valentino was born in Italy in 1879. He came to America in 1913 and worked as a gardener and dishwasher before coming to Hollywood to work in the movies. He shot to stardom in the 1921 film *The Four Horsemen of the Apocalypse*. He became a sex symbol and starred in films where he swept women off their feet, like *The Sheik*, made in 1921.

The newspapers suggested that, despite the fact he was a sex symbol, he might be gay. They pointed out that both his marriages failed, that he wore perfume and plucked his eyebrows. There is no evidence that this was the case, but the newspapers loved a scandalous story. Valentino died from appendicitis in 1926. There were 50,000 people at his funeral. Several women committed suicide because of his death.

► **Rudolph Valentino reading his fan mail.**

GLORIA SWANSON

Gloria Swanson was one of the great female sex stars of the 1920s. She starred with Rudolph Valentino in the film *Beyond the Rocks*, made in 1922. In some scenes she wore over a million dollars' worth of jewels!

In 1924 she married a French count. She later said that the public, 'rejoicing because Cinderella had met her prince', would have been much less pleased if they had known that she was pregnant at the time. She went through a patch of retiring from movie-making and then staging comebacks.

In 1929 Miss Swanson began an affair with Joseph Kennedy (father of John F. Kennedy, who became President in 1960). Kennedy poured large sums into Gloria Productions Limited, a film company which Miss Swanson had just started. But in 1930 the affair came to an end in an argument over money. She died in 1983.

CHARLIE CHAPLIN

Charlie Chaplin was born in England in 1889, into a very poor home. By 1913 he was in the USA, working in silent movies. He became a great comic movie star. Among his most famous films were *The Vagabond*, *The Gold Rush* and *The Pawnshop*. Later films were *Modern Times* (1936) *and The Great Dictator* (1942).

Chaplin had two failed marriages. An actress, Joan Barry, said he was the father of her child. Chaplin took her to court over this. The newspapers loved the scandal. Chaplin won the case, but some Americans turned against him and refused to go to see his films.

Chaplin was also unpopular for his political views. In 1952 Chaplin and his family went to live in Switzerland. Shortly before his death in 1977, he visited America to be given an award for his film making.

◀ **Charlie Chaplin in** *The Gold Rush*, **made in 1925.**

CLARA BOW

In 1921, at the age of sixteen, Clara Bow won a magazine contest and became a movie star. In 1927 she was the star of a film called *It*. Everyone knew 'It' was sex appeal. From then on she was known as the 'It' girl.

The newspapers were full of accounts of the scandalous things she did. She drove a red car, filled with seven dogs and sometimes a monkey – all dyed red to match her hair. She loved wild parties and had strings of love affairs. How much of the scandal that the newspapers dug up about her was true it is hard to say, but she was certainly wild.

In 1930 Miss Bow's secretary sold the newspapers the story of her employer's life. The secretary was later jailed for theft, but the damage was done. Clara's career was wrecked and she had a nervous breakdown. She tried a comeback but failed. She retired from film making in 1933 and died in 1965.

During the 1920s it seemed to people in other parts of the world that they were struggling to make ends meet, while Americans lived a life of luxury. The sources on these pages give examples of that 'American luxury'. But some of them also show that perhaps things were not quite what they seemed.

Source 1

Our New Radium $5.00 Home Permanent Wave Bathing Beauty

COPYRIGHT 1924 H.W. CHERRY

▲ A 1925 advert.

Source 2

▲ A 1927 car advert.

Source 3

◀ World goods produced in the United States.

Source 4

Number of millionaires in the United States:

1914   7,000
1920   35,000

Source 5

▲ From an American magazine, Christmas 1928. The unemployed father pulls his son away from the shop window. His son asks 'Will you be working by next Christmas, Papa?'

Source 6

	Average hourly wage of factory workers	Cost of a Model T Ford
1909	19cents	$950
1917	32cents	$440
1920	55cents	$360
1923	57cents	$298
1926	59cents	$290

Source 7

People say 'money can't buy everything' but many Americans in the 1920s thought it could! They scrimpd and saved to buy things to have 'the good life'.

Mr A. had to show he was better than Mr B, not by what he did or said, but by how many cars he had, the size of his house, and his wife's fur coat.

▲ Written by Harriet Ward, a modern historian.

QUESTIONS

Be sure to explain your answers to each of the questions below.

1 What do Sources 1 and 2 tell you about life in America in the 1920s?

2 Which of Sources 1, 2 and 6 shows best how wealthy America was then?

3 'Source 3 just shows what was made. It doesn't show if people were rich.'
Explain why you agree or disagree.

4 'Source 5 is about how well-off or badly-off some Americans were.'
Explain why you agree or disagree.

5 Look at Source 6.
When was it easiest to buy a car?

6 What did the writer of Source 7 think about life in the USA in the 1920s?

7 Do these sources prove most Americans in the 1920s were 'living the good life'?

CHAPTER 3

THE USA IN THE 1920s – THE BAD TIMES

There was a bad side to the economic boom of the 1920s. After the First World War, America turned away from the outside world. This policy is called **isolationism**. There were other problems too. Some Americans were well off. But many people, especially farmers, immigrants and black farm workers, never shared America's growing wealth. They still struggled to survive. There were also rising tensions between white and black Americans. There were bitter arguments between people who wanted change and people who did not.

3.1 Isolationism

What is isolationism?

Isolationism is when a country has as little contact as possible with the rest of the world. After the First World War many Americans wanted America to do this.

► This cartoon is from the British magazine *Punch*, published in 1919. The dove of peace is telling President Wilson that keeping world peace will be impossible.

Source A

OVERWEIGHTED.

PRESIDENT WILSON. "HERE'S YOUR OLIVE BRANCH. NOW GET BUSY."
DOVE OF PEACE. "OF COURSE I WANT TO PLEASE EVERYBODY; BUT ISN'T THIS A BIT THICK?"

Reasons for isolationism

Some Americans felt that America should not have joined in the First World War. They felt that 100,000 American soldiers had died fighting in a war that was really the business of Europe, not America. They argued that the American government should look after the American people and the American economy.

Rejecting the League of Nations

This is why America never joined the League of Nations, even though President Wilson had supported the idea. But the American Senate never accepted the Treaty of Versailles, which President Wilson had signed in 1919. If they had accepted it, the USA would have become one of the 'world's policemen'. Wilson led a nation-wide tour, trying to convince people that the USA should join the League. He failed.

This does not mean America had nothing to do with foreign affairs. The government tried to avoid getting involved in disputes that might lead to war. But they did try to help countries resolve disputes without war.

Keeping people out

As you saw on page 7, it was after the First World War that the USA began to restrict emigration to America. This was another example of isolationism. They were worried that too many immigrants would change the American way of life.

Source B

Americans would be fools to become involved in a European alliance. America promised to guarantee a stable peace. The peace cannot last. America should withdraw from all commitments which would limit her freedom of action.

▲ Why the United States should not accept the Treaty of Versailles. From the American magazine, the *New Republic*, 1919.

AMERICAN INVOLVEMENT IN WORLD AFFAIRS 1921-32

▶ **Washington Naval Agreements 1921–2:** The USA, Britain, Japan, France and Italy agreed a 10-year ban on warship building and limited the size of navies.

▶ **The Dawes Plan 1924:** The American Charles Dawes joined a team that helped sort out the German currency and lent $200 million to Germany.

▶ **The Kellog-Briand Pact 1928:** The US Secretary of State, Frank Kellog and French Prime Minister, Aristide Briand fixed an agreement where the great powers agreed not to fight each other.

▶ **Loans to other countries:** From 1924–8 the US lent $57 million to other countries (see graph, left).

▶ **The Young Plan 1929:** This reduced Germany's payments from the First World War and gave it longer to pay.

▶ **The Geneva Peace Conference 1932 and World Economic Conference 1933:** US representatives went to these conferences.

▼ American loans to other countries 1924–8 in millions of dollars.

1924	1925	1926	1927	1928
$968	$1,076	$1,125	$1,337	$1,251

Problems for the farmers

Almost half of all Americans either farmed or sold farmers the goods they needed. As food prices fell during the 1920s, millions of people were hit hard. Farmers did not do well in America in the 1920s.

Farmers had done well during the First World War. They had grown more crops to feed war-torn Europe. But when Europe could grow its own food again, American farmers had more food than they could sell. Three other things made matters worse:

• Many Americans ate less food that used grain.
• Farmers were using more and more tractors. These tractors replaced horses. The food that had been grown for horses to eat was now going to waste.
• It was hard to sell grain abroad. Other countries had put a tariff on American grain because of American tariffs on foreign goods (see page 12).

Many American farmers could not cope with earning less while having to pay out more. They sold up and moved to the cities to look for work. Some were thrown out of their homes for not paying their rent or their mortgages.

THE PROBLEMS OF FARMING IN THE 1920s

● In 1920 a bushel of wheat cost 233 cents. In 1932 it cost 32 cents.

● In the 1920s six million people moved to cities from the country.

● From 1919-24 600,000 farmers went bankrupt. Most of their land was left unfarmed.

● Most workers' pay went up in the 1920s. Many farmers made two thirds less money by the end of the 1920s.

▼ A poor farming family in the 1920s.

Source C

Employment of black Americans

Farmers with problems sacked their workers. In the southern states many farm workers were black people. In the 1920s, 75,000 black farm workers lost their jobs. Many black families had to move to the cities in the north to look for work.

When they reached the cities, most of these families ended up living in slum areas. The only jobs they could find were poorly paid jobs that did not need special skills, often in factories. Most factory workers worked long hours in appalling conditions for low pay. In 1929, a worker had to make at least $48 a week to keep his family. Most factory workers earned less.

Workers' troubles

Factory owners were doing well. But many of them wanted to do even better – by getting their workers to do more work for as little pay as they could. To do this, the factory owners had to act against any group that wanted a fair deal for workers. They did this by jumping on the first sign of any trouble. This became know as the 'American Plan'. It only worked because workers needed jobs so badly.

Factory owners crushed workers' organisations – like the **trade unions**. They broke up strikes with force. The Government also hammered the unions. Workers were earning less and less all through the 1920s. The gap between what they earned and the price of what they made got wider and wider.

QUESTIONS

1 Read pages 22–3.
 a What is isolationism?
 b How was America isolationist after the First World War?
 c How do you think the cartoonist in Source A felt about isolation? Explain your answer.

2 Read pages 24–5. Chose either farmers or black Americans. Explain how they suffered in the 1920s.

3 Read pages 25–6. What problems did workers face in the 1920s?

▼ A poor black family with their possessions in the 1920s.

Source **D**

Strikes

In 1919 the coal-miners of West Virginia went on strike. The state governor sent the army in to break up the strike. In 1927 cloth workers went on strike. The police arrested the strikers.

Workers began to think it was not worth joining a trade union, as the unions could not make things any better. In the 1920s, union membership fell from 5,000,000 to 3,600,000.

Government measures

So the unions could not help the workers. And the government would not. Both federal and state governments were against improving working conditions and wages.

Some states tried to help. They were stopped. The Supreme Court said it was illegal to set a minimum wage for women workers, and against the constitution to pass state laws against child labour.

3.3 Racism and Black Rights

White prejudice

During the 1920s many Americans were hostile to immigrants and black people. The most shocking examples of this was the way black people were treated

Source E

▲ Ku Klux Klan members in their ceremonial white robes. Even small children were brought up to believe in Klan ideals.

in the southern states. Many black Americans were descended from people brought to America as slaves. In 1865 slavery was abolished, but black people were not treated as equals. In southern states, where most black people lived, laws kept black and white people apart. Black people could not go to the same schools, eat in the same restaurants or even ride in the same railway carriages as white people. In most southern states they could not vote or serve on juries.

The Ku Klux Klan

The Ku Klux Klan believed White, Protestant America had to be saved from black people, immigrants, Jews and Catholics. They used extreme violence against people from all these groups, especially black people. Klan members swore an oath of loyalty to the USA and promised to defend the USA against 'any cause, government, people, sect or ruler that is foreign to the country'.

Source F

Father James Coyle, a Catholic priest in Birmingham, Alabama, was shot on his front porch. His killer, Edwin Stephenson, pleaded self defence. He said they had argued about Stephenson's daughter becoming Catholic. Coyle hit Stephenson, who shot Coyle to save himself.

Stephenson's daughter said Stephenson had threatened to kill Father Coyle. Coyle's sister heard no argument before the shot was fired. Forensic scientists proved Coyle had been sitting when he was shot. The defence lawyer played on anti-Catholic feelings in the jury. He also pointed out that Stephenson's daughter was married to a coloured immigrant, and so was far from reliable!

Stephenson was found not guilty. A former governor of Alabama said, 'We have not moved on very far from barbarism if murder can be justified by the religion of the victim'.

▲ The story of Father James E. Coyle, murdered in Birmingham, Alabama in 1921.

What did the Ku Klux Klan do?

The Klan held meetings where members wore white hoods and robes, and carried blazing torches. Klan victims might be told to leave town for their own safety. Others would be beaten up or have their houses or businesses burned down. The most terrifying punishment was to be lynched (beaten up and hanged).

In the state of Georgia there were 135 lynchings from 1924-5. No one was ever tried for these murders. In some towns policemen were members of the Klan. So were some judges and politicians. In the south it was hard to find a jury which would convict Klan members, or witnesses to give evidence against them.

Many Klan supporters were Whites who were competing with black people for unskilled work. They resented black people for making work harder to get. By 1924 there were an estimated five million Klan members. Some were even elected to Congress.

Source G

It is the way of the world that each race must fight for its life, must conquer or accept slavery or die. The Klan wants every state to make sex between a white and a black person a crime. Protestants must be supreme. Rome shall not rule America. The Roman Catholic Church is un-American and usually anti-American.

▲ The Klan's leader (Imperial Wizard), Hiram Wesley Evans, speaking in 1924.

Less support for the Klan

After 1925, fewer people joined the Klan. Klan members were involved in several political scandals. Some of them ended up in prison, although not for the harm they did to black people.

The Klan did not die out. There are still members in some areas today. But it was never as important again as in the early 1920s. By 1929 its membership had dropped to 200,000.

Fighting back

Black people set up groups to push for improvements for Blacks in America. Two famous black leaders were William Du Bois and Marcus Garvey. They both wanted better treatment of black people. But they did not agree about how to get this.

William Du Bois helped set up the National Association for the Advancement of Coloured People (NAACP) in 1910. He wanted America to accept all people, with equal opportunities for all.

Marcus Garvey thought black people should not try to be part of white society. He said they should celebrate their blackness and African past. In 1914, he set up the Universal Negro Improvement Association (UNIA). Garvey told black people to set up their own businesses, using only black workers. By 1920, the UNIA had over 2,000 members. UNIA groups wore military uniforms, and scared the government, who wanted to stamp them out. In 1923 they had Garvey put in prison for 'postal fraud'. When he was released, he was **deported** – forced to leave the country. Without him, the UNIA fell apart.

Du Bois said that Garvey was 'either a lunatic or a traitor'. He thought Garvey's attitude lost white support for the black cause. Garvey accused the NAACP of being 'the greatest enemy of the Negro' because of its belief in integration, which he felt would never work.

Source J

Marcus Garvey (1887-1940). He is wearing his UNIA uniform. Garvey's slogan 'Black is beautiful' had a big effect on many people who had been brought up to see being black as being inferior.
◀

Many Americans were against immigration to keep out people who had dangerous political ideas – like **communists**. Communists wanted everyone to share work and money equally. This did not fit in with American ideas of getting ahead by hard work. In 1919 some people feared a communist revolution was about to break out (this had just happened in Russia). They called for a crack down on people with 'un-American' political beliefs.

Sacco and Vanzetti

In May 1920 two Italian immigrants, Nicola Sacco and Bartolomeo Vanzetti, were arrested for armed robbery and murder. There was hardly any evidence against them. At the trial, people said they had seen Sacco and Vanzetti somewhere else when the crimes were committed. But they were **anarchists** (they did not believe in organised government). This turned the judge against them. They were found guilty and executed, despite protests all over the USA. They were really executed for their political beliefs, not for any crime. The judge later said to a reporter 'Did you see what I did to those anarchist bastards?'

The 'Monkey Trial'

It was not only political ideas that were seen as dangerous. Six US states banned the teaching of **evolution** – the idea that people had developed from apes. Christian fundamentalists in these states said children should be taught that God created people, as it says in the Bible.

In 1925 John Scopes, a biology teacher, deliberately broke the ban. He was taken to court. In the 'Monkey Trial' that followed his lawyers made fundamentalists look foolish and ignorant. Newspapers all over America followed the case. Most Americans laughed at the fundamentalists arguments. Scope was found guilty, but was not fined or put in prison.

Source K

Governor Dukakis marked the 50th anniversary of the executions by making 23 August 1977 'Sacco and Vanzetti Day'. Dukakis said 'the atmosphere at their trial and appeals was full of prejudice against foreigners and hostility towards unorthodox political views'.

▲ Part of *Sacco and Vanzetti*, a book written by the modern historian, Paul Avrich.

Source L

Before the judge stopped the cross-examination, Scopes' lawyer made the fundamentalist leader admit that he believed that Jonah had been swallowed by a whale and that Joshua had stopped the sun.

People in court roared with laughter.

▲ Part of *Anxious Decades*, a book written by the modern historian, Michael Parrish.

QUESTION

What did Christian fundamentalists want taught in schools?

In 1919 the United States Congress passed the Eighteenth Amendment to the American Constitution. Sometimes called the 'Volstead Act', it banned making or selling alcohol in the USA. This was also called 'prohibition'.

Early prohibition

Some states already had rules about selling alcohol. Some states, like Maine, had banned it all together. Prohibition had nearly been introduced in 1914, but did not have quite enough support.

Prohibition was a victory for those who believed the 'demon drink' was causing all the country's problems. They thought that men would spend more time at home and not waste their wages on drink.

All in favour?

Not everyone agreed with prohibition. Many Americans treated the new law as a joke. They turned avoiding the police and going for a drink into a game. So almost every night millions of Americans were becoming 'criminals'. Prohibition made drinking secret and exciting.

Gangster organisations now sold most alcohol, not shopkeepers. They set up **speakeasies** (illegal bars) where **bootleg** (alcohol brought into the country from abroad) or **moonshine** (alcohol made illegally in the USA) were sold. They made a fortune.

Source M

Two agents, Izzy Einstein and Moe Smith were famous for their methods. Izzy once sat, looking frozen, outside a speakeasy. Moe carried him in and demanded 'Give this man a drink! He's just been bitten by frost'. When the kindly bartender gave him a drink, they arrested him and closed the place down.

▲ Part of *Anxious Decades*, a book written by the modern historian, Michael Parrish.

Source N

▶ A cartoon published by the Anti-Saloon League. It is called 'The downward path'. It shows how drinkers lose control of their lives through alcohol.

State reactions

Some states, like New York and Wisconsin, abolished their laws against the alcohol trade. They said the Volstead Act was too extreme, and the Government would have to enforce it themselves.

Prohibition agents

Prohibition was very hard to enforce. The Government made John F. Kramer the Prohibition Commissioner. He had 3,000 agents whose job was to stop people selling alcohol. They did not get much help from the public. And they had to tangle with the gangsters who wanted to keep on making money.

Gangsters

Many gangsters were very rich. They could bribe almost anyone, from the local police officer to the highest police chiefs, judges or politicians. It was hard to resist the huge money bribes. If people did refuse bribes, gangsters often used to blackmail or violence to get their way. During the 1920s more than 500 prohibition agents were killed. Shoot-outs between gangsters and the police were common. Gangsters fought each other, as well. On 14 February 1929, the Chicago gangster Al 'Scarface' Capone murdered seven members of a rival gang. This became known as the St Valentine's Day Massacre. He wanted to keep hold of his share of the alcohol trade. In just one year, 1927, Capone made about $105 million.

The end of prohibition

Prohibition did not cure America's social problems. It led to more violence. Prohibition made many people lose their respect for the law. In 1933 President Roosevelt signed the Twenty-first Amendment **repealing** (cancelling) the Volstead Act. After he had done so he joked, 'I think this would be a good time for a beer'.

Source O

▲ A customer knocks on the door of a speakeasy. Speakeasies were hidden away in hard-to-find places.

Source P

Conditions are very bad. Corrupt public officials turn a blind eye, and everyone drinks – including underage boys.

▲ Report from a prohibition agent in Indiana, 1929.

QUESTIONS

1 What was prohibition?

2 How reliable is Source N for a study of attitudes to prohibition?

3 'Prohibition was silly. It caused nothing but trouble in the USA.' Explain why you agree or disagree with this statement.

Al Capone was born in Naples, in Italy, in 1899. Soon after this, his parents emigrated to America. At the age of 18 he had his face slashed by a knife in a fight over a girl. The cut was deep and the scar never went away. This is how he got his nickname, 'Scarface'.

Al Capone began his life of crime by running errands for a Chicago gangster called Jim Colosimo. Chicago had lots of gangs. At different times they worked together or fought each other.
In 1920, Colosimo was murdered by the Torrio gang. Capone could act with Colosimo's gang, and try to get back at the Torrio gang. Or he could change sides. The Torrio gang offered him the best deal. He became Torrio's second in command. When Torrio was hurt in a gang attack in 1925, Capone took over as leader.

Capone had to have a 'legal' job. He could not tell the tax people he was a gangster, even though everyone knew he was. He set up as a second-hand furniture dealer. He even had an entry in the phone book for secondhand furniture. But if anyone rang to buy furniture, they were told, 'We ain't open today'.

Capone's opponents said he had hundreds of men killed in his career. This is probably an exaggeration. But he did have people killed. It was an important part of gang life to be tough. It was also important to do things with 'style'. Capone once had a rival gang leader killed, then sent $50,000 of flowers to his funeral. Capone knew it was dangerous to be a gang leader. He had a bodyguard. He was careful about who he met. His car had so much armour plating that it weighed over seven tons.

▲ **Alphonse Capone (1899-1947).**

Capone was so famous that reporters discussed his public and private life as if he were a top movie star. In 1928, after years of trying to 'get' Capone, the government finally managed to arrest him. But not for any of his 'real' crimes. They prosecuted him for not paying his taxes. Capone complained bitterly, 'They finally got me for spitting on the sidewalk'.

Capone paid the $50,000 fine. He went to prison for eleven years. He was released in January 1939. By then the age of the gangsters was over. After his release he seems to have lived a quiet life until he died in January 1947, aged 48.

Source A

If people didn't want beer and wouldn't drink it, a fellow would be crazy for trying to sell it. I never saw anyone point a gun at a man and make him go in a gambling house. I've always seen it as a public service to provide decent liquor and fair gambling.

▲ Al Capone speaking in the 1920s.

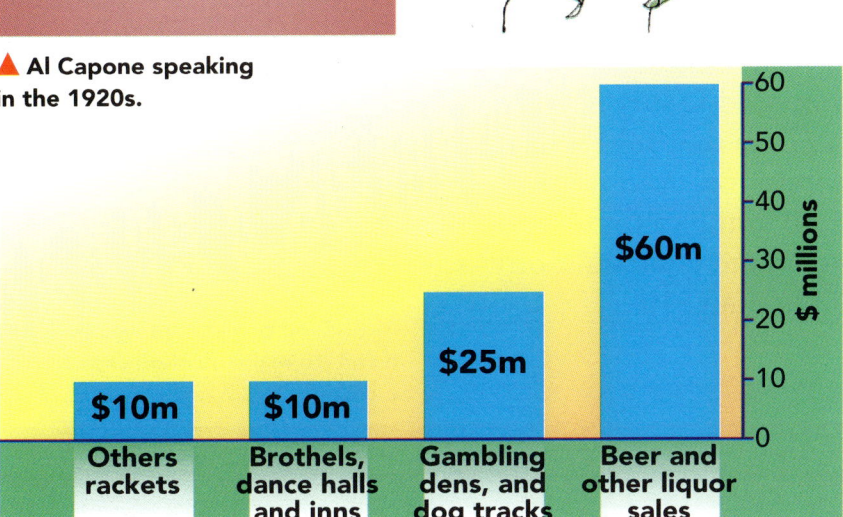

▲ Profits made by Al Capone in 1927.

Source C

Capone paid the hospital bills of a woman bystander wounded in a street gun-battle. He set up the first soup kitchens and block restaurants for the distribution of free food on Thanksgiving Day.

▲ Comment by a modern historian on Al Capone. His book tries to change the way people look at the prohibition gansters.

▼ Victims of the St Valentine's Day Massacre in 1929.

Source B

QUESTIONS

1 List all the ways Al Capone made profits.

2 Which sources and information would you use if you wanted to show Capone as a ruthless criminal?

3 Which sources and information would you use if you wanted to show Capone as a kind businessman?

4 What do you think of Al Capone? Use the information on these pages to support you.

It was almost impossible to enforce prohibition in the United States. It was a law most people did not support. There were plenty of people prepared to sell alcohol, despite the law. They were taking a risk, but making huge profits. The alcohol industry made about $2 billion for the gangsters who controlled the trade. They were not going to let 3,000 prohibition agents earning $2,500 a year stop them.

There were plenty of people prepared to buy alcohol, too. In New York the number of bars that sold alcohol doubled during the time of prohibition. And if you didn't want to drink in public, all you had to do was go to your local hardware store where you could buy home-brewing equipment for less than $10.

Source 2

We shall see that liquor is not made, sold, or given away, nor carried from place to place by land, under the earth or by air.

▲ Promise made by John Kramer, first Prohibition Commissioner, in 1921.

▼ Federal prohibition agents with a still (to make alcohol) captured in a cellar in 1925.

Source 1

Source 3

Prohibition agents were mostly inefficient and underpaid.

With whatever help they could get from state and local authorities, they had to patrol 18,000 miles of coastline. They had to stop the theft of 57 million gallons of industrial alcohol (used in medicines and household cleaners) and check hundreds of millions of doctors' prescriptions.

They also had to check 20 million houses to prevent home-brewing of wine or 'bathtub gin'.

▲ Written by a modern historian.

FACT BOX

● Prohibition agents found 130 gallons of illegal alcohol on a farm in Texas. The farm belonged to Senator Sheppard who proposed prohibition in 1919! He did not know about the alcohol.
● Someone did not like the taste of his moonshine alcohol. He asked a chemist to analyse it. The chemist said 'From the sample of urine you gave me, I would say your horse is sick'.
● Even when prohibition enforcement was at its toughest, Americans could still buy a drink in most major cities within one minute of stepping off a train.

QUESTIONS

1 Use the sources and your own knowledge to answer these questions.
   a What did Federal agents have to do?
   b How did people get alcohol anyway?
   c How did prohibition make the drink problem worse?

Source 4

An estimated 10-15 million gallons of alcohol, meant for use in for hair tonics, make-up and paint, got turned into bootleg alcohol each year. They had names like 'Parisienne Solution for Perspiring Feet, 90% Alcohol'. One bootleg drink was 'Sterno'. Doctors and coroners saw plenty of cases of drinkers killed by drinking it.

As for imported alcohol, in 1925 a government official said that his agents probably seized about 5% of all liquor smuggled into the United States each year. Samuel Bronfman, head of the Canadian distilling industry, thought it was less, 'though I never went to the other side of the border to count the empty Seagram's bottles'.

▲ Part of *Anxious Decades*, a book written by the modern historian, Michael Parrish. Seagram's was a brand of alcoholic drink made in Canada.

Source 5

► This 'flapper' shows how to conceal alcohol.

CHAPTER 4

THE USA AND THE STOCK MARKET CRASH

In November 1928 Herbert Hoover, became President. In October 1929 the Wall Street Crash – the collapse of the economy – happened. Some Americans had seen the Crash coming. They could see company profits were falling, while share prices were too high. But for most people the Crash was a terrible shock. Thousands of investors and stockbrokers lost money and many banks had to close.

The time that followed is called the Depression. Hoover tried to deal with the problems, but he did not believe the government should take direct action.

Hoover expected businesses to solve the country's economic problems. Little was done to help the unemployed. Hoover believed that people should help themselves, not rely on others.

4.1 What was the Wall Street Crash?

The American **stock market**, where shares are bought and sold, is on Wall Street, in New York. In 1928, share prices were still going up. Most people were still confident about the economy. President Hoover told Americans that poverty would soon be wiped out. During the summer of 1929, company profits began to fall. Share prices were still going up. This was because people were still buying shares, expecting prices to go on rising. But if that confidence disappeared people would stop buying shares. Prices would tumble and investors would lose huge sums of money.

Source B

We in the United States are nearer to beating poverty than we have ever been before in the history of our country.

▲ President Herbert Hoover speaking in 1929.

▼ Front page of the *New York Times*, 15 July 1928.

Source A

SPECIAL FEATURES
AUTOMOBILES

The New York Times.

SPECIAL FEATURES
RADIO—AVIATION

Section 9

Copyright, 1928, by The New York Times Company

SUNDAY, JULY 15, 1928.

NATION-WIDE FEVER OF STOCK SPECULATION

Eager Buying Has Reached All Classes of People Throughout the Country and Has Set New Records In Many Directions—Effects of Struggle to Grasp Profits in Trading in Securities Are Evident

And that is exactly what happened. Investors who sold their shares before October 1929 saved their money. But thousands of others were ruined by the collapse of share prices in what historians call the Wall Street Crash.

The panic starts

By early September 1929, company profits were clearly falling. But people still bought shares, so prices still went up. But it could not last. People could not ignore the continuing fall in profits. On Monday 21 October the stampede to sell shares began. So many shares were sold that the 'ticker' (the machine which shows share price changes as they happen) was 1.5 hours behind the actual changes in price. And all the prices were falling.

The banks act

A group of bankers decided they had to stop prices falling. They bought shares to push the prices up. They spent about $30 million of the money in their banks. At first it seemed that their rescue had worked. But it soon became clear they had wasted the money. As one historian recently said, 'It was like trying to empty Niagara Falls with a bucket'.

No confidence

Instead of keeping calm, people lost their heads and were desperate to sell. Their confidence had gone.

On 29 October over 16 million shares were sold. Prices tumbled and continued to drop for the next two weeks. People lost huge amounts of money. Some small investors lost everything.

Source D

World
FINAL NEWS EDITION

Market in Panic as Stocks Are Dumped in 12,894,600 Share Day; Bankers Halt It

Outside J. P. Morgan & Co.

▶ The *World* newspaper headline on 25 October 1929.

Why did the Crash happen?

As in most events in history, there is no simple answer to this question. There are many causes.

- **Overproduction** American industry was churning out more goods than it could sell. Only middle and upper class people could buy cars and electrical goods. By 1929 most people who could afford these things had bought them. As sales fell, profits fell. Share prices were bound to fall.

- **Rich and poor** More than half of the people in the United States were very poor. There was a big gap between rich and poor. No matter how easy it was to buy goods, the poor simply could not afford to buy them.

- **No export market** The government had put tariffs on foreign goods (see page 12). Other countries did the same to the USA. This made their goods expensive abroad. It was also hard to sell to other countries because they had not had an economic boom. They could not afford American goods.

CRASH FACTS

- Brokers actually fought each other to sell stock on the Exchange. Brokers lost shoes, spectacles, false teeth and even a wooden leg in the scramble.
- When the singer Eddie Cantor asked for a hotel room the manager asked, 'Sir, will that be sleeping or jumping?' because of the many suicides.
- A messenger boy bought shares in the White Sewing Machine Company for $1 a share. The company did not collapse. He became a major shareholder in an important American company.

Source F

We are the first nation in the world to go to the poor house in a car.

▲ Said by an American writer in 1931.

Source E

If a man saves $15 a week and invests in good shares he will have at least $80,000 at the end of 20 years. He will get $400 a month, too. I believe that anyone can be rich, and they ought to be.

▲ John Raskob, a capitalist, speaking before the Crash.

Source G

Company	Before (3 Sept)	After (13 Nov)
General Electric	3.96	1.68
U.S. Steel	2.79	1.50
Standard Oil	0.83	0.48
General Motors	1.83	0.36

▲ The share price (in dollars) of four of America's big companies before and after the Wall Street Crash.

- **Over-confidence**
  Share prices rose in the 1920s because people thought shares were a good, safe way to make money. Because lots of people wanted to buy shares, prices went up.

  In the 1920s many more small investors bought shares. In 1920 there were 4 million people who had shares. In 1929 there were 20 million. But many of these people did not understand the risks they were taking. They believed prices would never fall.

THE WALL STREET CRASH: TIMETABLE TO DISASTER

3 September 1929: factory profits begin to fall.

5 September 1929: first fall in share prices.

6 September 1929: continued buying on the margin helps the market to recover.

21 October 1929: prices begin to fall sharply.

24 October 1929: panic on Wall Street. 13 million shares are sold. $9 billion is wiped off share values. Banking syndicate spends $20–30 million buying shares to keep prices up.

29 October 1929: 'Black Tuesday' After several steady days the market collapses. Over 16 million shares are sold.

12 November 1929: prices still falling. The market has fallen 40% since mid October.

Why did everyone try to sell at once?

People panicked for several reasons. Those who did not understand how share prices worked felt that once they fell, they would go on falling. They did not realise that if they waited, prices would stop falling.

Most people just could not afford to wait, anyway. They had bought shares 'on the margin' (see page 13). They had borrowed money to buy shares. They had to make a profit to pay off their loans. So they panicked and sold their shares as quickly as possible before prices dropped even more.

Once the market began to fall, lots of people began to sell. This brought down share prices. More people panicked and sold shares. Prices went down more. In a way, people desperate not to lose money put themselves in a position where they were sure to do just that. A vicious circle of panic selling had set in.

SUMMARY

Causes of the Crash

- **Overproduction**: more goods were made than could be sold.

- **Uneven wealth**: too few people had the money to buy goods.

- **Lack of export markets**: tariffs and lack of wealth abroad prevented American goods being sold abroad.

- **Over-confidence**: people were borrowing money to buy shares.

- **Panic**: investors sold when the market began to fall. They could not afford to make losses. This forced prices down.

The immediate effects

- The big investors in Wall Street were rich Americans. Many of them lost everything in the Crash. They could not afford to buy luxury goods anymore. They were selling them instead. And they were forced to sell at ridiculously low prices – because there were very few buyers around.

- Most of the new investors in the 1920s were investing small amounts. Their losses were small, compared to the amounts lost by big firms. But it was all they had. Some people never recovered.

- The reason the Wall Street Crash made such a big impact on the American economy was that big and small investors had been borrowing money to buy shares. They owed money to banks and stockbrokers. Some stockbrokers and financial advisers were ruined. They threw themselves from office windows and died on the streets below.

THE CRASH: IMMEDIATE EFFECTS

Within one year of the Crash:

Wages down $4 billion

The value of goods made dropped from $87.8 billion to $75.7 billion

Unemployment up from 1.3 million to 4.3 million

659 banks closed

Source I

Some people put their houses up for sale. It was useless – no one was buying. So they boarded them up and left. One old couple who lived near us lost everything in the Crash. It was too late for them to start again. They committed suicide.

▲ A young American remembers life during the time immediately after the Crash.

Source H

$100 WILL BUY THIS CAR MUST HAVE CASH LOST ALL ON THE STOCK MARKET

◀ People sold whatever they had for whatever they could get.

- Banks were in a bad position too. They had lent money to buy shares. They had lent money to invest in businesses. They had bought shares themselves. They tried to get their money back from people they had lent money to. Customers who had money in the banks began to lose faith in them. They took their money out. In the same way as the share panic spiralled, now a bank panic set in. More and more people took out money. Banks were forced to close. Customers who still had money in those banks lost it. Some people had their life savings wiped out.

- The Wall Street Crash destroyed the confidence which had set off the 1920s boom. People with money kept it. They did not buy shares or goods.

The banks that survived the Crash stopped lending money. The money needed to keep industry going dried up. Companies cut production, laid off workers and reduced wages. The good times were gone and the Great Depression was just beginning.

QUESTIONS

1 What was the Wall Street Crash?

2 Explain how these three contributed to the Crash
   • over production in factories
   • government tariffs on foreign goods
   • panic selling of shares.

3 How did the banks try to save the economy?

4 Why was it so damaging when these groups of people were hit by the Crash:
   a rich investors
   b ordinary people
   c banks?

5 'In some ways, loss of confidence in shares and the banks was the cause of the problems.' Explain why you agree or disagree with this statement.

6 Who were worst hit by the Crash, big or small investors? Explain your answer.

Source J

◀ *Club Life in America: the stockbrokers.* A cartoon from *Judge* magazine, from November 1929.

The long-term effects

Some Americans thought the Wall Street Crash was a short-term crisis that the country had to 'ride out'. It soon became clear this was not the case. The USA plunged into the deepest depression it had ever known.

After the Crash people bought fewer goods. This led to a downward spiral where profits fell and workers were laid off. So people wanted fewer goods. So more workers lost their jobs. By 1933, 100,000 companies had gone out of business. The banks could not help. From 1930–33, even though they had survived the first bank panic, 3,400 more banks closed.

Source K

▲ People flocked to eat free soup in Pittsburgh in the early 1930s.

Rising unemployment

In 1928 there were about 2.5 million unemployed people in the United States. By 1933 it was almost 13 million. In some places it was worse than in others. Some cities had over 75% of the people living there unemployed.

Hoovervilles

Many unemployed people could not pay the mortgage or the rent on their homes. They became homeless. They set up shanty towns on the edges of many towns and cities. These were called 'Hoovervilles', after President Hoover, because many people blamed him for not trying to stop unemployment.

Demand for goods drops

Company profits fall

Workers laid off

Less money to buy goods

Demand for goods drops

◄ The downward spiral of economic depression.

How to eat?

At this time, the government did not think it was their job to help people who had no money, or who lost their jobs. People were expected to look after themselves. If people had no wages coming in, they had to live off money they had saved. If people had no savings, they had to rely on charity for food or anything else. Men who, during the 1920s, had made the United States a rich country now queued for free bread and soup.

The struggle to survive

Mass unemployment put an enormous strain on many people's family lives. Some tried to scrape a living by selling matches, apples or pencils. There were more prostitutes on the streets as desperate women tried to raise money. Some people begged to make money. Others lived on food and things they found thrown away on rubbish dumps. Some even turned to crime to feed their families.

Some men became 'hobos' – taking free lifts on trains to go around the country looking for work. Thousands of people were brought to hospital with **malnutrition** which was caused by not having enough food to eat. Many of these people died. Americans in the 1920s would never have believed that in the 1930s hundreds of American people would die of starvation.

Source L

The rubbish dumps in Chicago are haunted by the hungry. Last summer in the hot weather, despite the sickening smell and the flies, a hundred people a day came to one of the dumps. One widow who used to do housework and laundry, but now has no work, feeds herself and her 14 year old son on rubbish. Before she picks up the meat, she takes off her glasses so that she cannot see the maggots.

▲ An American reporter describing what he saw in Chicago in 1933.

▼ A 'Hooverville' in Central Park, New York.

Source M

From bad to worse

Farmers had found it hard to make a living in the 1920s. The 1930s were worse. People bought less food. Shops and food companies cut prices to try to sell more. So they paid farmers less. Many farmers went bankrupt and were thrown out of their homes. They loaded up their trucks and drifted into towns looking for work.

The weather makes things worse

To make matters worse, there was a drought in the midwest. Because of the lack of water, the soil blew away in dust storms. Millions of acres of farmland became useless. This part of the country became known as the **Dust Bowl**. Thousands of farmers packed up and set off for other parts of the country, like California, looking for work. Few of them found it.

A world-wide effect

The Depression in America affected the rest of the world, too. After the First World War, America had lent about $6,000 million to other countries. Now it wanted some of this money back. When countries, like Germany, had to pay the money back their own economies went into a depression.

Source N

Figures cannot tell the whole story: they leave out the terrible effects the Depression had on countless people up and down the country.

There was the old man who sees his life's savings vanish; the ragged child surviving on one skimpy meal a day; the young wife who watches her energetic husband become, idle, then irritable, then scared, then just listless.

▲ From *The Effects of the Depression, America Since 1920*, by the modern historian, D. Snowman.

▼ Unemployment in the United States 1929-1933.

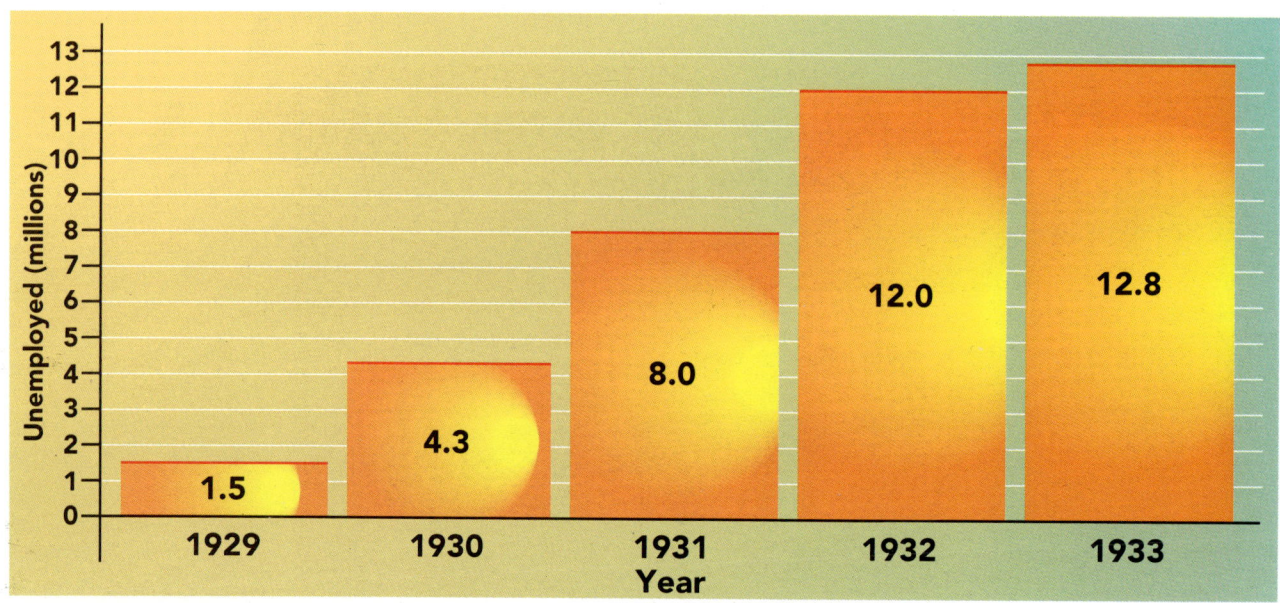

Source O

◀ A family fleeing from poverty in the Dust Bowl between Dallas and Austin, Texas in 1936.

FARM PRICES 1919–32

	1919	1929	1932
Cotton ($ per pound)	.353	.167	.065
Wheat ($ per bushel)	2.160	1.030	.380
Corn ($ per bushel)	1.510	.790	.310

QUESTIONS

1 Explain how the downward spiral (see page 42) caused the Depression.

2 If you could use just one of Sources L and M to show the effects of the Depression, which would you use? Explain your answer.

3 You have to give a radio talk. You have 75 seconds to sum up how the Depression affected EITHER factory workers OR farmers.

Source P

◀ A 1932 picture called: 'Breadline. No one has starved'.

When Herbert Hoover was elected President in 1928 America was rich. Hoover said 'We want a nation of home owners and farm owners. We want to see their savings protected. We want to see them in steady jobs'. He had no idea how hard it would be to do this.

Reaction to the Depression

No one at the time realised how long the Depression would last, or how bad it would get. America had had depressions before. The last one had been in 1921. The economy had recovered without government help. Not only did the country recover, the 1920s became a boom time. Many American economists thought the 1929 Depression should be handled in the same way.

What was *laissez faire*?

Hoover was a Republican. Republicans thought the government should not interfere in people's lives, even to help. This policy was called '*laissez faire*' – which means 'leave things alone' in French.

Laissez faire and business

The Republicans thought governments should not tax businesses heavily or fix minimum wages. If a company was efficient and sold its goods at the right price, it would make money. If it was not, it would fail.

Laissez faire and unemployment

Republicans believed that a person was responsible for his or her own life. If the government paid unemployment benefit or tried to create jobs they would destroy the American way of life. They thought government 'interference' was what happened in Communist countries, not in the world's greatest democracy.

Support for Hoover

In early 1929 most Americans would have agreed with Hoover and the Republicans. But it became clear that the Depression was not going to turn around. People needed help. They were angry with Hoover for not doing anything to help. A banner carried during a protest march in 1932 summed up many peoples' attitudes: 'In Hoover we trusted and now we are busted'.

◀ Herbert Hoover (1874–1964), American President 1929–33.

So what did Hoover do?

Was Hoover a hard-hearted President who ignored the worst aspects of the Depression? No. He believed it was wrong for the government to pay unemployment money or create jobs. But he tried to get other groups to help.

How did he help?

In 1929, Hoover signed the **Agricultural Marketing Act**. This helped farmers to work together to become more efficient. In 1931 he set up the **Reconstruction Finance Corporation** (RFC) to help finance companies and banks. In 1932 state governments and city councils ran out of money to help the unemployed. Hoover told the RFC to lend them up to $300 million to keep people in jobs.

Law and order

Hoover's *laissez faire* ideas did not extend to law and order. In 1932, thousands of people who had fought in the First World War marched to Washington. They wanted their ex-servicemen's bonus (due in 1945) to be paid early, to help them through the Depression. Some marchers set up 'Bonus' camps in the city.

Hoover called in the army. The 'Bonus campers' were driven out of the city with tear gas and fixed bayonets. Their camp was then burned to the ground. Hoover claimed the marchers had been stirred up by Communists. Few people believed this. Treating ex-servicemen and their families like this made Hoover very unpopular.

MEASURES TAKEN BY PRESIDENT HOOVER

In 1929
- Hoover tried to reassure the American people by saying that the Depression would not last long. Most business leaders agreed with him.

- Hoover called business, farm and union leaders to Washington. These leaders agreed to work together to beat the depression.

- Hoover cut taxes by $160 million and asked Congress to give him the huge sum of $423 million dollars to undertake public works.

- Hoover encouraged Congress to pass the Agricultural Marketing Act which set up the Farm Board. It was given $500 million to help farmers.

In 1930
- Hoover agreed to put higher tariffs (taxes) on foreign goods to make them dearer for Americans to buy.

In 1931
- Hoover set up the Reconstruction Finance Corporation (RFC) to help finance companies and banks in difficulty. During 1932 it lent $1.5, mostly to banks.

In 1932
- Hoover told the RFC to spend up to $300 million to provide shelter, clothing and food for the unemployed.

- He signed the Emergency Relief and Construction Act which spent $1.5 billion on public works schemes.

4.6 Exercise: Herbert Hoover – does he deserve the criticism he has attracted?

Herbert Hoover has been greatly criticised for his failure to take extreme measures to deal with the Depression. But is that criticism really fair?

Source 1

Many Americans in 1929 saw an economic depression as something that was bound to happen now and then, like a rainstorm.

The nation's bankers felt it was sensible to let the depression run its course. Nothing could be done about it, so nothing should be tried.

It was inevitable after such a prosperous time.

◀ **From a book about the Depression by a modern historian.**

Source 2

Unemployment can be cured by making jobs. You represent the business of the USA. You should help our economy.

This is not interference by the government with business. The government is asking you to co-operate in sensible measures to solve a national problem.

▲ **Extract from a speech made by Hoover to a group of business leaders in December 1929.**

Source 3

American society, Hoover believed, depended on the moral fibre of its people. He had worked his way from a poor childhood to success and wealth. So could others. He argued that 'the spread of government destroys initiative and so destroys character'. He believed that no effort to defeat the Depression should go against the fundamental ideas of American society – people relying on themselves.

▶ **From a study of Hoover, 1929.**

Source 4

▲ **'While Washington makes up its mind....' A cartoon printed in the United States in 1932. It shows the Senate unable to decide what help should be given to the unemployed.**

Source 5

Today we are living in a
   shanty
Today we are scrounging for
   a meal
Today I'm stealing coal for
   fires
Who knew that I could steal?

I used to winter in the tropics
I spent my summers at the
   shore
I used to throw away the
   papers
I don't any more.

▲ **Extract from the song 'We'd like to thank you, Herbert Hoover'. The song was written in the 1980s for the show, 'Annie' (set in 1932). In the show it is sung by homeless people huddled around fires trying to keep warm.**

▲ **Children at one of the Bonus camps with anti-Hoover posters in 1932.**

QUESTIONS

1 List the sources on these pages under two headings:
   a critical of Hoover
   b sympathetic to Hoover.

2 Read **Measures taken by President Hoover** on page 47. What <u>did</u> Hoover do to help?

3 Why didn't Hoover do more to help America pull out of the Depression? Use the sources on these pages and read pages 46–7.

4 Use the information on pages 46–7 and the sources in this exercise. Which of the statements below seems most accurate to you?

'President Hoover was a hard-hearted man. He deserves the criticism that has been made of him'.

'Herbert Hoover was just unlucky. He was elected at the wrong time. There was little he could do. No one else would have done any better'.

CHAPTER 5

ROOSEVELT AND THE NEW DEAL

President Roosevelt swept to power in the 1932 election. His message was: 'The American people want two things: work and security. I pledge myself to a New Deal for the American people. Help me to restore America to its own greatness.' Roosevelt knew he had to act quickly to build confidence in the economy and get people back to work.

Roosevelt's policies were so popular that he was re-elected three times. He was seen as the person who turned the country around. Yet many people claim that the New Deal was an expensive mistake. They argue that the USA came out of the Depression because of the outbreak of war in Europe, not because of Roosevelt's policies.

5.1 Why did Roosevelt win the 1932 election?

Time for a change?

By 1932 it was clear that the Republican President Hoover was not dealing with the problems caused by the Depression. He was very unpopular with millions of Americans. People wanted a change. But Hoover and the Republicans did not want to change their policies. They felt they would only ruin government finances and destroy the American way of life by putting government money into creating jobs.

A different view

Hoover's opponents, the Democrats, were pushing for change. Their election candidate was the Governor of New York, Franklin D. Roosevelt. He was rich, clever and an excellent public speaker. He was sure that America needed government help to get people back to work. Some Democrats were not sure how it was to be paid for, but Roosevelt promised to introduce a 'New Deal' to get Americans back to work.

Source A

▲ Roosevelt (on the right) on the campaign trail.

Source B

This is more than a political campaign, it is a call to arms. Help me not only to win votes, but to restore America to its people. Millions of Americans hope their old standards of living have not gone for ever. They cannot and shall not hope in vain. I pledge you, I pledge myself to a New Deal for the American people.

▲ Roosevelt's speech to the Democratic Party shortly after being made its candidate for the 1932 election.

Source C

Smile away the Depression!

Smile us into Prosperity!
wear a
SMILETTE!

This wonderful little gadget will solve the problems of the Nation!

APPLY NOW AT YOUR CHAMBER OF COMMERCE OR THE REPUBLICAN NATIONAL COMMITTEE

WARNING—Do not risk Federal arrest by looking glum!

Voting for the New Deal

The American voters had little doubt which of the two candidates they preferred. They rejected Hoover's calls for moderation and 'wait and see' policies. They had been waiting. Things had just got worse and worse.

Instead they voted for Roosevelt – the man who promised to take action. Roosevelt won the election easily.

Elections to choose representatives in the House of Representatives and the Senate (who worked together in Congress) were held at the same time as the election of the president. Most of those elected were Democrats, Roosevelt's party. Now Congress, where Federal laws were made, was full of Democrats. It was time for the New Deal.

QUESTION

Why do you think Americans chose to vote for Roosevelt, not Hoover, in the 1932 election?

◀ An American newspaper cartoon published in 1932.

▼ A modern historian's thoughts on Hoover's 1932 campaign.

Source D

President Hoover warned people that if the Democrats won 'The grass will grow in the streets of a hundred cities, a thousands towns: the weeds will overrun the fields of millions of farms'.

He said the election was a contest between two rival ways of government and that Roosevelt was 'proposing changes and so-called new deals which will destroy the foundations of our American system'.

On 4 March 1933, Roosevelt took office. He had promised the American people a New Deal and now set about putting his policies into action.

Restoring confidence

In the 1920s, America had been rich and confident. America in 1933 was an entirely different place. People were frightened of unemployment, of homelessness, of poverty. Roosevelt knew he had to make people confident again. He also had to get people who had money spending again – or at least putting their money back in the banks.

Faith in the banks

The day before Roosevelt took office, two more banks shut. The banking system was in danger of collapse. Roosevelt ordered all banks to close. Using the Emergency Banking Act, he sent in people to inspect the banks' accounts. Only banks that were not likely to collapse were allowed to re-open. No banks were allowed to trade in shares with their customers' money. So people had confidence in the banks again.

Fireside chats

Roosevelt used the radio to talk to the American people. Shortly after his election he began a series of broadcasts, which became known as 'fireside chats'. He explained, as simply as possible, how he would solve the country's problems. He talked as if he was a friend in the room with them. He even talked about his family and his pet dog, Fala. Many people felt that here, at last, was a President who cared about about them and shared their worries.

Source E

The only thing we have to fear is fear itself – terror which paralyses our efforts to change retreat into advance. This nation asks for action, and action now. Our biggest task is to put people to work. This problem can be solved if we face it wisely and courageously.

▲ Part of Roosevelt's first speech as President, made to the American people in March 1933.

▼ Roosevelt speaking on the radio in 1932 in one of his 'fireside chats'.

Source F

▲ The symbol of the National Recovery Administration.

► President Roosevelt explaining the reason for the NRA Blue Eagle Badge.

In a war, in the gloom of night attack, soldiers wear a bright badge so they do not fire on each other. Those who co-operate in this programme must know each other at a glance. We have provided a badge of honour for this purpose, a simple design with the legend 'We do our part'.

Helping those in need

Roosevelt set up the Federal Emergency Relief Administration (FERA) to help the hungry and homeless. $500 million went to help states to look after the poor. Money went on nursery schools, soup kitchens, blankets and setting up jobs. Roosevelt cut the pay of people who worked for the government to fund this. He also used taxes from the drinks trade, now prohibition was over.

Keeping a roof over their heads

Roosevelt set up the Home Owners Loan Corporation (HOLC) to help people who had problems paying the mortgages on their homes. It took over mortgages from banks and allowed people to repay them over a longer period of time.

Better conditions for workers

Roosevelt set up the National Recovery Administration (NRA) to improve working conditions for those people with jobs. The government set maximum hours of work, minimum wages and outlawed child labour. Factory owners and workers in the scheme had to agree on fair prices and working conditions.

No firm had to join the NRA, but 2.5 million firms did. They could then use the Blue Eagle symbol of the NRA. People knew these firms were 'good' firms. But some of them did not always follow their own codes. In 1934 the NRA was replaced with the National Labour Relations Act. This forced employers to accept trade unions. Firms often fought against this, but by 1939 union membership had risen from 3.3 million to 9 million.

The Social Security Act

The Social Security Act of 1935 said that from 1940 the government would give pensions to workers aged 65 and over. The government raised the money to pay these pensions by setting up special taxes that workers and employers had to pay. The government also agreed to help state governments set up unemployment benefit, sickness pay and help for the disabled.

Roosevelt said that the Social Security Act summed up what the New Deal was all about – helping as many people as possible to live full and useful lives.

▶ 'Priming the pump'

1. **Government sets up schemes to create work**
2. **Workers are paid**
3. **Workers spend wages on goods**
4. **Factories make more goods**
5. **Factories need more workers**
6. **Workers are paid**

Work creates more work.

Creating employment

Roosevelt's most important task was to create work for the huge numbers of unemployed. He believed that people had to start spending money to get the economy going. They did not have money to spend, so the government had to create jobs. When people began to earn wages they would spend them. People would want to buy more goods. Factories would need more workers, to make more goods. Then there would be more people with money to spend. The economy would recover without any more government help.

The Alphabet Agencies

Roosevelt asked Congress to pass the 'Alphabet Laws', setting up Alphabet Agencies (identified by the first letters of the key words). Their main aim was to find work for the unemployed.

Was everyone happy?

There were some complaints about Roosevelt's policies. Taxes went up to pay for them. Some people complained about having to pay for the jobs that were created.

SUMMARY

Roosevelt's first measures – 1933

▶ March   Roosevelt takes office
▶ March   FERA set up
▶ March   Emergency Banking Act
▶ March   First of 'fireside chats'
▶ March   Civilian Conservation Corps set up
▶ May   Agricultural Adjustment Act passed
▶ May   Tennessee Valley Authority set up
▶ June   Public Works Administration set up
▶ June   NRA set up

The Agricultural Adjustment Administration (AAA) (1933)

In 1933 about 18 million acres of land were taken out of cotton and wheat production by the AAA, to stop overproduction. Tobacco growing and animal rearing were also cut.

Control of production helped to raise farmers' incomes. At the same time the AAA provided finance to modernise farms and improve farming techniques.But these measures caused unemployment for farm labourers.

The Civil Works Administration (CWA) (1933)

The CWA provided instant employment for those out of work. In its first four months it spent $933 million setting up over 180,000 work schemes. It lasted a year, then was replaced by the WPA. In one year it provided work for 4 million unemployed. It built 800,000 kilometres of roads, 40,000 schools and employed more than 50,000 teachers.

The Civilian Conservation Corps (CCC) (1933)

The CCC provided 6 months work for unemployed 18-25 year olds. People worked on countryside conservation – planting trees and digging canals. Workers were paid $1 a day and had to send home $25 a month. This was a very popular scheme. During the 1930s nearly 2.5 million men served in the CCC.

The Public Works Administration (PWA) (1933)

The PWA was given $3,300 million to spend on public works to create jobs. It cleared city slums and built new housing. It built new schools, sewage plants, hospitals, bridges, city halls and courtrooms. The PWA also produced new war planes and airfields for the Army Air Corps and built two aircraft carriers, *Yorktown* and *Enterprise*, for the navy.

The Tennessee Valley Authority (TVA) (1933)

The Tennessee Valley was one of the poorest areas in the country. It was called the Dust Bowl and there was high unemployment.

The TVA covered 41,000 square miles across seven states. It built twenty major dams and a system of inland waterways. It planted millions of trees to bind the soil. It set up new farms. Businesses, and even tourists, came to the area.

The Works Progress Administration (WPA) (1935)

The WPA co-ordinated the work of all the job creation agencies. It was responsible for smaller-scale projects and found work for about 3 million unemployed. The WPA spent $11 million setting up projects like improving hospitals and schools, and building playgrounds. It also supported artists and writers.

Historians disagree about the success of the New Deal.

Evidence of success

Rising confidence People were more confident. They put their money back in the banks. They felt the government was helping them.

Farmers were making more money. They were getting government help to pay their mortgages and other debts.

Employment 'Priming the pump' had boosted production and increased employment. The Alphabet Agencies had got the federal government and the states working together to bring down unemployment. People could now get unemployment benefits and old age pensions. Millions of workers now had the protection of trade unions.

Source I

A promised land, bathed in golden sunlight, is rising out of the grey shadows of want and wretchedness down here in the Tennessee Valley now.

▲ A Tennesse resident talking about the effects of the work of the Tennessee Valley Authority, one of the 'Alphabet Agencies'.

▼ A description of the men who worked on a Civilian Conservation Corps project by Arthur Schlesinger, a historian writing in 1959.

Source J

They planted trees, made reservoirs and fish ponds. They cleared beaches and camping grounds and protected and improved parks, forests and recreational areas.

They came from large cities, from small towns, from slum street corners, roads, railway tracks and from nowhere. Their muscles hardened, their bodies filled out, their self-respect returned. They learned trades; more important they learned about America and other Americans.

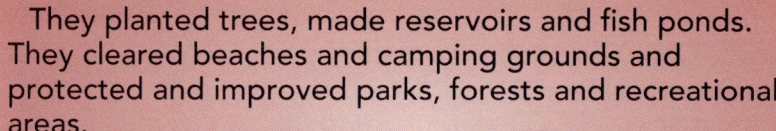

▼ Number of unemployed in millions, 1929-41.

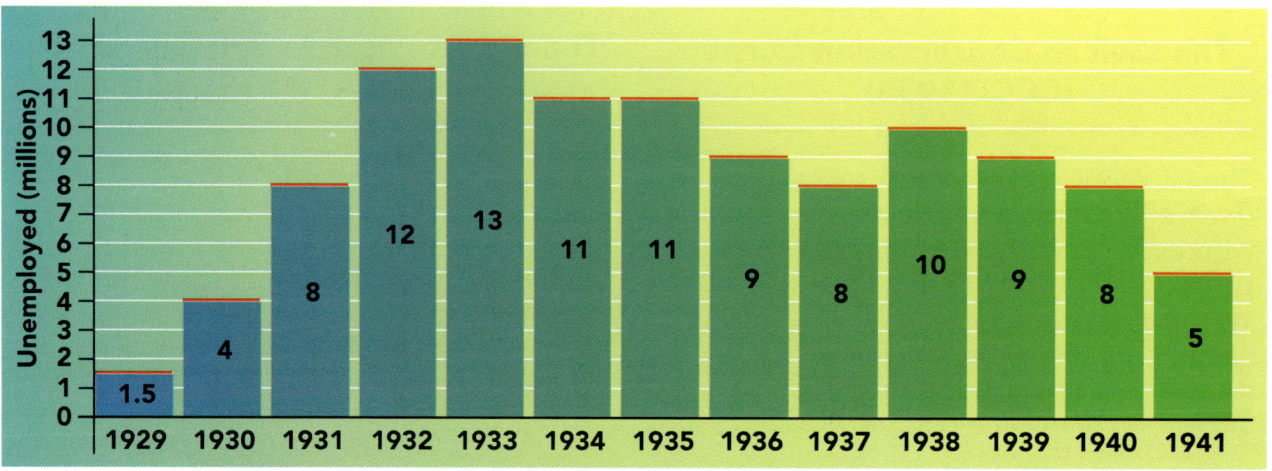

Source K

The New Deal left many problems unsolved. It even created new ones. As late as 1941 there were still 6 million unemployed. It was not until the war years of 1943 that the army of jobless finally disappeared. The New Deal made a more just society, but left many Americans (slum dwellers, mostly negroes) outside. Some of these omissions were remedied. When recovery did come it had a sound base because of the New Deal.

▲ The view of William Leuchtenburg, a historian writing in 1963.

Evidence of failure

Farmers were getting better wages, but were still very poor. The Dust Bowl was still a big problem.

Unemployment By 1937, unemployment was around 8 million. This was over 4 million less than in 1933, but still over five times more than in 1929.

Taxes Government reforms were mainly paid for by higher taxes. Americans in well-paid jobs were paying higher taxes than ever before.

In 1937 the American economy hit another depression. Unemployment rose. The government was spending more than it was getting in taxes. So it cut spending.

When unemployment reached 10 million Roosevelt had to ask Congress for huge sums to create jobs. Congress agreed and the economy once more began to pick up. But it looked as though the economy could not really keep itself going without government help.

Source L

▲ A cartoon published by Roosevelt's opponents during the New Deal.

War – the real reason?

It seems likely the New Deal would have ground to a halt. Then, in 1939, the Second World War broke out in Europe. American industry sold war goods worth millions of dollars to the Allies. The armed forces took on men in case the USA joined the war. This was the 'kick-start' the American economy needed. When the Japanese bombed Pearl Harbor in December 1941, the USA entered the war to fight on the side of the Allies. Shortly afterwards unemployment fell below the level of 1929.

QUESTION

Do you think the New Deal was a success? Explain your answer.

Roosevelt was re-elected in 1936, 1940 and 1944. He joked that everyone was against him except the voters. Why?

Republicans

Many Americans, especially Republicans, did not believe in spending government money to create jobs. They did not agree with interfering in how businesses were run, or letting workers join trade unions. Roosevelt's opponents said people should look after themselves. The government should not find them jobs, or give sickness benefits and old age pensions.

▶ This so-called 'Confidential Report on the Condition of the Nation under the New Deal' was issued by an American company in 1936. It was making fun of Roosevelt's measures.

Source N

Population of United States	124,000,000
Eligible for Old age pension	30,000,000
That leaves to do work	94,000,000
Working for government	20,000,000
That leaves to do work	74,000,000
Forbidden to work by the Child Labour Law	60,000,000
That leaves to do work	14,000,000
Number unemployed	13,999,998
That leaves to do work	2

ME AND THE PRESIDENT
HE HAS GONE FISHING
AND I'M GETTING DAMN TIRED

Source M

THE ILLEGAL ACT.

PRESIDENT ROOSEVELT. "I'M SORRY, BUT THE SUPREME COURT SAYS I MUST CHUCK YOU BACK AGAIN."

Farming matters

Paying farmers to produce less food while some people starved seemed immoral to some Americans. Others thought it just made the farmers lazy. One critic told farmers they might just as well 'shoot their cows and milk the government'.

◀ A cartoon in the British magazine, *Punch*, in June 1935 reacting to the Supreme Court's ruling that the NRA was illegal.

Too much government power?

The Tennessee Valley Authority co-ordinated the work of seven states. So the federal government was telling seven separate states what to do. Many people felt this gave the federal government too much power. In 1935 the US Supreme Court declared the NRA (see page 53) was against the American Constitution. It said the President was not supposed to make rules about employment. Roosevelt tried to appoint new judges to the Supreme Court, saying some of the judges were too old. What he was really trying to do was get his suporters into the Supreme Court, which was supposed to be impartial. Many Americans argued against this. Roosevelt dropped the idea. But it had damaged his reputation.

Not enough help?

While some people thought Roosevelt had gone too far, others said he had not gone far enough to help the poor. Some of them set up their own political parties. One critic, Father Charles Coughlin, set up the National Union for Social Justice.

Another opponent, Dr Francis Townsend, organised old people to press for better pension rights. He lost support when one of his most important officials was caught stealing funds. The loudest and most colourful of Roosevelt's critics was a member of his own party, Senator Huey Long of Louisiana.

QUESTIONS

1 Why did the Republicans criticise Roosevelt?

2 What point was the author of Source N making?

3 Do you think the cartoonist in Source M supported or opposed the NRA? Explain your answer.

4 'Roosevelt must have been unpopular. Even people in his own party turned against him.' Explain whether you agree with this statement.

Source O

Look at this NRA they opened two years ago. Everything from a peanut stand to a power station has a book of rules. A little fellow who ironed trousers went to jail for charging 5 cents less than the prices in the rule book. They've got 900 codes. It would take 40 lawyers to tell a shoeshine stand how to operate and not go to jail.

▲ Huey Long, speaking in the Senate in 1935.

Source A

▲ Huey Long (1893–1935) punching home a point.

Source B

Huey believed everybody in politics had a skeleton in his cupboard.

By showing he could find and open cupboard doors (and make trivial mistakes seem greedy or evil) he tried to make the Senate do as he wanted.

▲ A modern historian describing Huey Long's tactics.

Source C

Huey was like a horsefly. He'd land on part of you and sting you. When you slapped him, he'd fly away, land and sting you again.

 Senator Alben Barkley of Kentucky, describing Huey Long.

Huey Long was the son of a poor farmer. He saw himself as the leader of the poor whites in the South and the enemy of big business. He was a powerful speaker who could manipulate crowds. He loved insulting his opponents, calling them 'thieves', 'bugs' or 'lice'.

Governor and Senator

In 1928, Long was elected Governor of Louisiana. As he said to his supporters 'Now we'll show them who's boss'. He meant the big businesses.

In 1930, Long was elected to the Senate. He helped Roosevelt become the Democratic Presidential candidate in 1932, and supported the New Deal. But he turned against Roosevelt's policies, criticising him for not doing enough to help farmers. He said Roosevelt helped the banks more than the unemployed. He gained a lot of support. Roosevelt was dismayed to hear that Long was going to stand against him to become the Democratic Presidential candidate in 1936.

'Share-Our-Wealth'

In February 1934 Long announced plans to provide every family with $5,000 by taxing the rich. No one could have over $5 million in savings, or earn more than $1.8 million. His opponents said that the sums did not work.

But if people pressed him about how his scheme could work, Long said 'Just shut your damned eyes and believe it. That's all'. He won a lot of support, especially among the poor, who wanted to believe that his 'Share-Our-Wealth scheme would work.

▶ A cartoon from the *Philadelphia Inquirer* showing Roosevelt laughing at Huey Long's political threats.

Source D

YOU AND ME ARE THROUGH!

HUEY

F.D.R.

Source E

Long used methods which even the most ruthless politician would think twice about.

Long appealed to wild extremists. He would have made himself a dictator if he could.

Some of his programme was sensible. Roosevelt decided to adopt those parts of it. He said, 'Maybe we had better try to steal some of Huey's thunder'.

▲ A modern historian's view of Huey Long.

Long's dream ends

Long's dreams to become the President who shared out America's wealth came to a dramatic end. He was assassinated in 1935. Although many politicians were glad to see the end of a dangerous rival, his death was dreadful blow to the people of Louisiana. About 175,000 people went to his funeral.

QUESTIONS

1 Why did Huey Long stop supporting the New Deal?

2 Who did Long appeal to?

3 Why did this make him a dangerous opponent?

4 One historian has said Huey Long's 'Share-Our-Wealth' movement showed his good side and his bad side. What do you think he meant by this?

Source 1

▲ Soil erosion in Tennessee Valley in the early 1930s.

▼ From the *Report of the Government Committee on Unemployment in the United States, 1932.*

Source 2

One day my father took me to a Hooverville. It was ten miles wide and ten miles long. People lived in old rusted-out car bodies. I mean that was their home!

Some kids made shacks out of orange crates. One family with a whole lot of kids lived in a piano box. A family with seven kids lived in a hole in the ground.

▲ Peggy Terry recalls life in Oklahoma City in the early 1930s.

Source 3

In the last 3 months I have visited 20 states. In Montana people said thousands of bushels of wheat were left uncut in the fields because its low price hardly paid for cutting it. In Oregon I saw thousands of bushels of apples rotting in the orchards. Yet there are millions of children who, because of poverty, will not eat one apple this year.

In Oregon the local paper told of sheep farmers killing sheep and feeding them to the buzzards because they cost more to take to market than they would fetch there. Yet in the same month I saw people picking for meat scraps in the garbage cans of New York and Chicago.

In this country we have reached the stage where we have over-production and under-consumption at the same time.

Source 4

People starved on the streets. A hospital doctor told me people fainted in streetcars every single day.

In the hospital they knew what caused it. When the patient was conscious, they'd feed him. People were flopping on the streets from hunger.

▲ A local doctor describing life in Chicago in the early 1930s.

Source 5

A generation of women has grown up believing that nothing is impossible if they were willing to work for it. More women went to work. More of them had important jobs.

Now these women have learned that nothing is certain. The Depression created a lost generation of girls who should have gone to work in 1929, but may never have a job. It is quite possible that women will be told to go home and leave the jobs to men. It is likely that the century-old woman's movement has crashed against the facts of the Depression.

▲ Part of 'Women and the Depression' published by the American Woman's Association in 1934.

Source 6

▲ Children in front of their run-down home, 1936.

QUESTIONS

1 Read Source 2.
  a Describe a Hooverville in your own words.
  b Why do you think Peggy's father took her there?

2 Why was food destroyed when people were starving (Source 3)?

3 Which of the sources in this exercise do you think gives the best idea of life in the Depression? Explain your answer.

INDEX

AAA (Agricultural Adjustment Administration, 1933) 55
Agricultural Marketing Act 47
Alphabet Laws 54, 55

Blacks 22, 25
  and rights 26, 28
Bonus marchers (1932) 47
Bow, Clara (film star) 19

Capone, Al 31, 32–33
car industry 10–11, 15, 38
Carnegie, Andrew 7
Charlie Chaplin (film star) 15, 19
Christian Fundamentalism 29
  and the 'Monkey Trial' 29
cinema 15–16
CWA (Civil Works Administration 1934) 55
Constitution of The United States 8, 59
communism 29, 47

Dawes Plan (1924) 23
Democrats 50–1, 60
Du Bois, William 28

economy 5, 56–7
  and First World War 5
    'boom' 10–12, 41, 46
    farming 24–5, 55, 56–7
    Wall Street Crash 36–7, 39, 40–41
  (see also Great Depression)
Emergency Banking Act (1933) 52

factory workers (see industry)
farmers 5, 22, 24–5, 44–5, 55
FERA (Federal Emergency Relief Administration) 53
First World War 5, 10, 11, 22, 23, 24
  and women 17
Ford, Henry 11, 25

Garvey, Marcus 28
Government 8–9
  Federal 8, 59
  State 8, 26, 30, 31, 59
Great Britain 5, 8

Great Depression 36, 41, 42–4, 46, 50
  and banks 41, 42
    President Hoover 42, 46
    farmers 44–5
Greta Garbo (film star) 15

Hays Code 16
HOLC (Home Owners Loan Corporation) 53
Hollywood 15, 16, 18–19
Hoover, Herbert, (US President) 36, 42, 46–9
  and 1932 election 50–1
'Hoovervilles' 42–3, 62

immigrants 6–7, 22–3, 26, 29
  and 'Open Door' 7
Immigration Acts (1921, 1924) 7
Indians 6
industry 10–12, 38
  and mass production 10
    outbreak of Second World War 57
    workers conditions 25–26, 53
    trade unions 25–6, 53, 56, 58
isolationism 22–3

Jazz Age 15

Kellog-Briand Pact (1928) 23
Klu Klux Klan 26–7

'laissez-faire' 46
League of Nations 23
Long, Huey 62–3

NAACP (National Association for the Advancement of Coloured People) 28
National Labour Relations Act (1934) 53
NRA (National Recovery Administration) 53
New Deal 50–4, 56–7, 58–9, 60

poverty 43
President of US 8
prohibition 30–1, 34–5
PWA (Public Works Administration, 1933) 55

radios 10, 14, 15, 52
Reconstruction Finance Corporation (1931) 47, 48
Republican party 46, 50
Roosevelt, Franklin D., (US President) 50–60
  and 1932 election 50–1
    'fireside chats' 52
    opposition to 58–9, 60
    'priming the pump' 54, 56,
  (see also New Deal)

Sacco, Nicola 29
St Valentines Day Massacre 31, 33
Scopes, John 29
Second World War 57
Social Security Act (1935) 53
speakeasies 30–1
stock market 13–14, 36–7, 39, 40
Swanson, Gloria 18
Supreme Court 8–9, 58, 59

taxation 12, 57
TVA (Tennessee Valley Authority) 55, 59
trade unions (see industry)
Treaty of Versailles (1919) 23

UNIA (Universal Negro Improvement Association) 28

Valentino, Rudolf (film star) 18
Vanzetti, Bartolomeo 29
Volstead Act (1919) 30, 31

Wall Street Crash (1929) 36–41
Washington Naval Agreements (1921–2) 23
women 10, 17, 43, 63
  'flappers' 16–17
  and the vote 17
Woodrow Wilson (US President) 23
WPA (Works Progress Administration) 55

Young Plan (1929) 23